Living On Your Own
by
Kathleen Kole

Homeworld

The Publisher:
Lone Pine Publishing
#206, 10426-81 Avenue
Edmonton, Alberta, Canada
T6E 1X5

Canadian Cataloguing in Publication Data
Kole, Kathleen
        Living on your own
(Homeworld)

Includes index.
ISBN 1-55105-018-8
1. Single people — Life skills guides. 2. Living alone.
3. Home economics. I. Title. II. Series.

HQ800.K64 1992 646.7'008'652 C92-091773-9

Original Compilation: *Keith Ashwell*
Editorial: *Lloyd Dick, Debby Shoctor, Gary Whyte*
Homeworld Editor: *Lloyd Dick*
Cover Illustration: *Linda Dunn*
Printing: *Friesen Printers. Altona, Manitoba, Canada*

The publisher gratefully acknowledges the assistance of the Federal Department of Communications, Alberta Culture and Multiculturalism and financial support provided by the Alberta Foundation for the Arts in the production of this book

Contents

So, You're on Your Own

With all of the experiences that each individual has to face in his or her lifetime, it seems that there is one common to all of us: moving out. It is a task both exciting, and frightening.

It is exciting because, for the first time, **you're** calling the shots. Your home truly is **your** home. On the flip side of that coin, "your home" can suddenly mean responsibilities about which you know nothing.

However, these responsibilities are not as overwhelming as they may first appear. In fact, as each one is met and accomplished, they can help to boost your own confidence in your ability to meet any challenge.

This book is a guide to help you in meeting your challenges, as you stand for the first time alone in your new home. Can you picture it? The friends and family who helped you to move have just closed the door behind them, you are surrounded by mountains of boxes and furniture, and now it's up to you to create some sort of order amidst the chaos. Where do you begin?

By picking up "Living On Your Own" of course! You have probably already dealt with tasks such as your hook-ups, etc. before you got to this point, but if not, don't panic. "Living On

Your Own" has covered all the bases, to help you move away from home and survive on your own as smoothly and successfully as possible.

Shall we begin?

Moving

Before you make it to "the moment of truth" and are standing in your new home amidst the boxes that contain your belongings, there were steps that helped you to get to that point. Obviously, packing those boxes was first on the list. This may sound like an easy enough task, however there are some details that need to be considered before you begin to pack that first box.

Packing

"How hard can it be?" you ask yourself: just open a box, put your life inside, close it, and away it goes to your new home. Stop! Before you have packed every last possession you own to take to your new home, consider a few things:

The size of your new home

If you are preparing to move into a Bachelor, one or two-bedroom apartment/townhome, you will want to streamline your list of "essentials." Before you start packing, it is advisable to first take inventory of what exactly you are carting along with you. For example, cutlery is essential, but it's quite possible that the twenty-five stuffed animals you won at the carnival are not. This, of course, is a judgement call that you will have to make on your own. The point here is to consider the amount of space that you will have available for storage, and pack accordingly.

What goes where?

When packing, it is a good idea to have a thick felt marker on hand. As each box is filled and closed, it can be marked immediately as to what room it belongs in. This saves a great deal of time when unpacking in your new home.

Oops! Was that glass?

When dealing with glassware, i.e. plates, cups, glasses, etc. you should be careful to pack these kinds of items to prevent breakage. One way is to wrap each item in newspaper, or any equivalent, and then stack them carefully inside your boxes.

Other than these tips, packing is just what it appears to be: Work! So, now that you have sorted through all of your "worldly possessions," and are on your way to having all of your boxes marked and ready for moving day, it's time to consider how you are going to get yourself and your belongings to the home you've decided to move to.

Who will make the move?

How to get there is usually the last thing that a person thinks of when he or she is preparing to move. Other issues such as where you are moving to, what kind of rental policy the owner has, installing your cable, and so on, seem to take precedence over thoughts of transporting your belongings to your new home.

However, this issue is the most important! What's the point of having cable if your T.V. isn't there to be hooked up! When considering how you are going to transport your things, you have two basic options: friends and family, or a professional moving company.

Friends and Family

If you know enough people who own large vehicles such as trucks, vans, etc., then it is very possible that your move could be completed without the assistance of a moving company. This is probably the first thing you should consider before looking to professionals to move you. However, if this option is not available to you, then you have to go ahead and find a moving company.

Moving Companies

The decision of which moving company to use can be difficult. Whom to trust to get the job done carefully and efficiently can be a job in itself.

Before turning to the phone book, you might first consider asking your family and friends who have used the services of a moving company which ones they would recommend. Find out who was professional and efficient, and who was not. As well, find out about the costs involved and compare. Perhaps someone you trust has a company that they have used and has proved to be a worthy prospect. This could save you a lot of wasted time thumbing through the phone book.

If you have to rely on the phone book, then again I stress: compare. Phone around until you feel that you are getting the best service at the best price. Remember, you are paying them. Make sure that you know exactly what their contract includes pertaining to possible property damage while moving and so on. You want your move to be as smooth as possible.

Well, now that the "how to get there" is secured, we had better double check on your new home.

Rental Agreements

When you are choosing your new dwelling, you not only have to agree with the carpeting, but the lease that your new landlord/resident manager presents to you. Make sure that you go over it carefully before making your decision. Certain things you might look for are:

Pets and/or Children

While you yourself may not have pets or children, it is important to know if either is allowed in your complex. Reasons for knowing this information can include the possibility that you want to stay in your new home for quite some time, and in future may decide to share your home with a pet. If pets are not allowed on the premises, this could make a difference in your final decision. As well, even if you plan to remain solo for quite some time, both children and pets can generate a fair bit of noise and disturbance that you may not wish to deal with. Be sure about the lease before you sign.

Move-in Allowance

Some apartment/townhome dwellings have a move-in allowance. This is an incentive to get you to move into the building by offering you credit for rent. Before choosing your new home, find out how much this allowance is, and whether or not you can apply it to your rent on the last month you reside in the complex, if and when you choose to move out.

Damage deposits are the opposite of this, requiring you to pay a deposit in addition to your first month's rent to give the landlord insurance on any damage you may cause to your apartment. Damages will be deducted from this amount when you move out.

Accommodation inspection report

It is important to do a thorough inspection with your landlord before you take up residence in your new home. This report will be a record of the condition of the apartment/townhome before you moved in. Therefore, when the time comes that you choose to move out, you cannot be held responsible for any damage or imperfections that may have been present at the time you moved in.

Security

Security is very important, and should be given great consideration before moving in. What kinds of locks are present on both the windows and doors is very important. Thieves often see apartments and basement suites as easy targets. Therefore, take precautions when choosing your new home. Always make sure you have the locks changed when you move into a new place. You can never be sure of how many sets of keys are floating around to the locks on your new doors. Getting the locks changed assures you that the only keys available to your doors are yours and your resident manager's.

Although most doors have a lock in the door handle, you may want to consider having a dead bolt put on your door as well. If an intruder is at your door, a dead bolt will give him/her a few minutes of trouble at least, giving the police time to respond to your emergency call. The same goes for a door chain. A peephole will allow you to see who is at the door before opening it, and can be an added security measure.

Now that wasn't so difficult was it? A few moments of your time put to use, and now you feel secure that you know what to expect when you move in. However, before you file that new lease away in the top drawer of you desk, there is one other issue of prime importance: your utilities. What are they? These things include your power, cable TV and telephone, and must be arranged by YOU — usually your resident manager has nothing to do with them. So, to avoid sitting in the dark in your cold new apartment, with no T.V. to watch, here are a few things to help you figure out how to get those utilities working.

Utilities

Where is that light switch... Ah, here it is... What's going on?...It's not working! How am I supposed to get anything unpacked if I can't see!

   This is probably a common predicament for most first-time singles. No one bothers to tell you that you have to get such things as your lights, power, and cable hooked up before you move in. Isn't it enough that you payed for the place and gave a move-in allowance? Do you have to worry about power too? Don't despair. Compared to all of the other tasks you've had to deal with, this one is relatively simple.

• **Phone installation:** Before you take up residence in your new home, you need to inform the phone company. This means either going to or phoning their nearest office and arranging to have your phone hooked up on the day that you move in. Be prepared to pay a fee — the phone company requires a payment from you as security that you will pay your bills. This fee applies only to those who have never had a phone line in their name, and will be returned to you after a time when you have proven yourself to be a trustworthy customer. Find out how much the fee is, and how long the time period is before you get your money back.

• **Power:** The city power company must also be informed of your residency in order to hook up your power. This can usually be taken care of at the same time as your phone, as both companies are often run by the city.

• **Cable T.V.:** If you desire to have cable hooked up to your T.V., you must first find out which cable company services your area. If you have just one cable company in your town or city, this will not apply. Once this has been determined, you must then contact the company and arrange to have a technician come to your home and hook up your cable. Sometimes you may have to be home when they do this, and sometimes they can do it without you. This service will require a fee from you, therefore it is best to inquire as to the cost when you contact the company.

Now you should be able to see that utilities are not nearly as intimidating as they first appear. They take little time and effort, but can save the trauma of reaching for the light switch only to be left sitting in the dark.

Now, on to the good part! Yes, we have finished the preparation, and we are now ready to move in!

When You First Arrive

Finally, you're in your new home! Just when you were ready to give up and raise the white flag in defeat, you persevered and now here you are. Take a look around, it's all yours! The kitchen, the bathroom, the bedroom — all yours to do with as you wish. So, let's get to it!

As you assess each room of your new home, it will become apparent that they will require different amounts of organizational time. For example, the living room will not require as much time as the kitchen, and so on. Therefore, it might be wise at this time to make yourself a chart that prioritizes each roomand how much time it will require:

Room Organizational Needs		
BATHROOM	Medicine cabinet and cupboards.	1/2 hour
BEDROOM	Furniture placement, closet space, pictures, dresser drawers, and so on.	3 hours
KITCHEN	Drawers and cupboards, fridge and food storage.	3 hours
STORAGE ROOM	Arranging least and most-used items for accessibility.	1 hour
LIVING ROOM	Furniture placement, pictures, lamps, plants, and so on.	1 1/2 hours
DINING ROOM	Furniture, china. in cabinet	1 hour

Remember that the above chart has been prioritized according to rooms, not the time each will take to organize. According to this chart, it is believed that the bathroom is more important to arrange than the dining rtoom, even though the dining room may take more time. Ultimately the decisions about your rooms will have to be yours to make. This chart is just a guide to help you make the organization of your home less overwhelming.

Storage

Now where did I put that thingamajig? Was it in here...no. Maybe in here, no...ouch, my head! There isn't enough light in here to see my own hand let alone that darn thingamajig! I really do have to get more organized and get rid of some of this clutter!

Your storage room is very much a part of the cleanliness of your home. Without it, your home would be littered with all of the things that you choose to keep out of sight, or only need on an occasional basis. Of course, you will not only be using your designated "storage room" for storage. The other rooms in your home such as the bathroom, kitchen and bedroom will also be used as storage space. Again, this is why it is so essential to use the space you have to its maximum potential.

The first thing to do when addressing the issue of storage, is to answer a few simple questions:

1. How often will the stored items be used?
2. What size are the items being stored?
3. What kinds of storage space do I need?

These kinds of questions are important to address before you begin to put your belongings away. Once you know the answers, then you can begin storing and not have to interrupt yourself when confronted with a surprising lack of space. Let's begin with your storage room.

Storage room

Storage or utility rooms vary in size. Each one will have both its benefits and drawbacks. The key here is to make the most of both. Here are some simple steps to follow when you begin your organization:

- Assess your storage room. What does it need to make it work for you? i.e. shelves, peg boards, etc.
- Visit your local hardware store for ideas. By taking some time to browse through the shelves at your local hardware store, you may find many different types of hooks, racks, peg boards and so on, designed to help organize your storage or utility room.
- Divide up the items that you use most and least often. Those used most often should be placed in the areas of most convenience. Those used least often should be placed out of the way, and stored so that they use the least amount of space.

Please also remember that if you are renting, whatever you put up must also come down when you choose to leave. Anything that attaches to the wall will leave a hole and must be repaired before you vacate your home. Often the best solution is to visit a hardware store and purchase some sort of filler that will not leave any marks upon the walls.

Now all that is left is putting these steps into motion! Just keep in mind that once you have your storage room organized and functioning for you, you must keep it that way. Otherwise you'll end up with a room that is not only cluttered, but also cramped with organizational items!

Bathroom

The bathroom in most homes is never big enough. Most often-heard complaints are that it is too small and doesn't have enough counter, closet and under-sink space. However, these problems can usually be solved quite easily as the kinds of items stored here are generally not that big. Again, if you are renting, then you must take into consideration the damage you will have to repair once you leave — most apartments or townhouses will not object to the installation of towel racks or other similar items. When you leave, these items enhance the appeal of the apartment or townhome for the next renter. However, if you are thinking of installing anything, it is advisable to check with your resident manager first.

There are many ways to deal with lack of towel or counter top space. These include:

- Installation of towel racks either on the back of the bathroom door or on the wall above your toilet.
- Inexpensive open-shelves that can be attached to the wall areas around the sink and over the toilet, or free-standing shelves. This not only gives you more towel and open storage space, it gives you a space which can be used to add accessories to your bathroom.
- Inquire at your local hardware store for additional ideas.

Keep in mind that you can always check with your resident manager about making changes. If you want to install another medicine cabinet at your own expense, you will often find that your manager is encouraging instead of sceptical. Once again, these additions enhance the appearance of the apartment or townhome and increase its renting potential.

Kitchen Organization

Some parts of your kitchen may organize themselves. For example, your cutlery tray may only fit in one or two of your kitchen drawers. This leaves you the quick decision of choosing which drawer is most convenient and closest to your working or cooking area.

Other areas of your kitchen may take some time and consideration before you begin. Such areas include the cupboards above and below the counter area, and, where applicable, the pantry. If you put some thought into the organization of these areas, the results can be a surprising increase in both storage and food space, and better accessibility to both your dishes and utensils.

Cupboards

First, divide up those items that you use the most and the least often. Then place your least-used items in the back of your cupboards, and the most-used in the front.

Cupboard storage

Self-adhesive hooks can be attached to your cupboard doors and used to hang such kitchenware items as strainers and graters.

Self-stacking containers are inexpensive and can be used as an efficient tool to help you store your dry goods such as pasta, beans, etc. While most pastas are sold in plastic, usually the package contains much more than you will require for an individual meal. By investing in containers, you will be saved the hassle of plastic bags that split open, finding twist ties to close them and loss of freshness due to improper storage.

Keep in mind that your used jam and jelly jars, as well as many other kinds of containers are also great for storage. Once cleaned, they are perfect for storing small quantities of foods that may lose their freshness if left in an unsealed bag.

Counterspace

Once you put your mind to it, you will find many different ways of effectively storing your kitchenware and food items. Just always keep in mind that the better organized you are, the more time it will save you in the long run.

One of the areas that is similar to the bathroom in annoyance level is counter space. No matter how much is available, it's never enough. This is caused primarily by clutter and inefficient use. There are many different ways to make better use of the counter tops in your kitchen. One of the best ways to find out what is available to help you is to go to your local mall and investigate the kitchen stores and the kitchen sections in the department stores. Here you will find an assortment of different items designed to organize your counter tops.

Cupboard Space

- Become familiar with your cupboards. Consider which are your biggest and smallest, and what kinds of items are most suited to each.
- Consider what you have in your cupboards. You probably have both kitchenware and food items. These can be placed according to the size of your cupboards to maximize upon space.
- Make better use of your space by adding organizational tools to your cupboards:

  • By inserting hooks to hang your cups on, you can open up a great amount of space that can now be used to store the saucers and so on.

  • You can purchase ready-made shelves that can be slipped into the space between the existing ones, thus creating more shelf space.

  • If your cupboard doors are sturdy, a few racks will allow you to store smaller items here, leaving the inner cupboard space available for larger items.

A few suggestions of what you might look at are:
- spice racks
- decorated jars and canisters for sugar, flour, etc.
- under-cupboard hanging appliances and hooks

These purchases not only help to eliminate clutter, but they can give a polished look to your kitchen.

Another way to remove clutter from your kitchen and maximize storage is to make use of the space on your walls. These three areas, when their potential is realized, can help to make your kitchen a pleasure to work in.

Kitchen walls

Now let's move on to your walls. They can be used for much more than hanging pictures or clocks. By ignoring their potential, you are depriving yourself of greater storage space and easier access to frequently-used items.

If you have ever had the experience of searching for a certain pot or pan, you will greatly appreciate the suggestions found here:

1. Invest in a peg board. The board can be used for hanging your pots and pans, cooking utensils, and any other items you may need at your finger tips.

2. Purchase several bar racks and a few ring holders. If you have a wall at least three inches wide, you now have a place to display your decorative dish towels. As well, you have omitted the problem of towels bunching up under the sink, and opened more space here for storage.

Yet again, I suggest that you scout around for ideas and visit your local department stores. The more you organize your kitchen, the easier you will find it to concentrate on cooking instead of searching for hard to get at items.

Kitchen Storage Ideas

CUPBOARDS:	- hooks for hanging cups - insert additional shelves - door racks
COUNTER TOP SPACE:	- spice racks - decorated jars and canisters for sugar, flour and so on - bread box - under-cupboard appliances and hooks
WALLS:	- peg board for pots, pans and utensils - bar racks and ring holders for towels
GENERAL:	- check local department stores

Cleaning and Washing

I'll be the first to admit that there doesn't seem to be very much that is exciting about cleaning. And, you may be inclined to skip this section altogether. But, before you start turning the pages, take a moment to read a statement in its defence: once you have finished the task of cleansing your living space, you will be able to hold your head high and proudly invite guests to walk through your door. Almost makes you want to read on and learn a few cleaning tips that Mom never taught you. Well, how about this: when Mom does come over, she'll have nothing to say because your home will sparkle almost as much as hers. So, grab a mop and let's get to it!

Cleaning tips Mom never taught you

"Clean up your room! Make your bed and pick up those clothes!" These statements and many more are probably familiar to you from your childhood. Well, she was right. She kept her home clean and fresh, and we were never embarrassed to invite our friends in!

One of the most efficient ways to approach cleaning is to devise a system. One such system is to make a list of the duties that need to be done daily, and those that can be done weekly, monthly or yearly. By using this course of action, you are prepared in advance and can plan your other activities around these chores. So, let's begin with your daily duties.

Daily:

1. Make your bed.
2. Wash the dishes.
3. Tidy up your living space; put away magazines, newspapers.
4. Wipe off kitchen counters.
5. Clean eating area.
6. Clean up any spills.
7. Empty ashtrays (where applicable).

You may have more of your own depending upon your personal situation. however, this is a list of the most common chores that need to be performed daily.

Weekly:

1. Clean sink, bath and shower area.
2. Dust and vacuum all rooms.
3. Wash kitchen, bathroom and entryway floors.
4. Wash all counter tops, fridge and stove tops, etc. in kitchen area.
5. Wipe down the T.V. and computer screens.
6. Empty all garbage cans and put trash out to be taken away.
7. Do the laundry, including sheets and towels.

Again, these are just some of the primary chores that need to be done weekly. Your list may include others according to your circumstances. It is also advisable once a month to give your refrigerator a complete cleaning, and to clean the inside of your stove or oven.

Yearly:
1. Clean kitchen cupboards.
2. Tidy closet space, give any old clothes or items you do not want any more to charity.
3. Re-organize storage areas if they have become messy.
4. Wash windows inside and out.
5. Wipe off telephone and other appliances.
6. Wash walls.
7. Clean all light switches and door knobs.
8. Clean outside windows, if possible.
9. Beat rugs and air out blankets and comforters.

Wait a minute, I think we are done here! This whole "cleaning thing" didn't take as long as we thought it would! In fact, if your daily chores ARE completed on a daily basis, your weekly chores every week, and so on, your entire cleaning routine should take only a minimal amount of time to complete. And, believe me, it's well worth it to invest the time. If you aren't convinced, try a one-week experiment. For one week do no cleaning at all. Just eat, watch T.V. and whatever else you normally do in your home. Upon completion of that week you will be very surprised at how grimy a home can get without regular cleaning.

Now we must delve more deeply into a specialized area of cleaning — your laundry.

Your first laundry load

What's the big deal? Laundry is like packing — toss everything into the machine, throw in a little soap, turn it on and sit back with a good book. Stop! I thought your mother had dealt with this "toss everything in together" problem before you even moved! Well, like packing, laundry needs to be sorted. But before we even get to separating your clothes, let's get you to the machines.

Depending upon the type of building you moved into, your complex may or may not have washing machines and dryers on the premises. If it doesn't, then it is important that you inquire with your resident manager or a neighbour as to where the closest laundry facilities are located.

Separating your clothes is a simple process once you understand the "why" and "how." The "why" is easy to answer. However, to some it is not fully understood until they experience what happens when you don't separate your clothes. Have you ever pulled your new white socks out of the washing machine only to find them a soft shade of pink or grey? This is a perfect example of why you should take the time to separate your laundry. Need I say more? I didn't think so. Now, the "how" is a fairly straight forward process:

Separating your laundry

- collect all of the clothes, towels, sheets and so on that you are going to wash.
- Check the labels for any items that may have special washing instructions — "dry clean only," "wash by hand," etc.
- Separate any clothing items that haven't been washed before. This is important because the colour in the material of the new item might run if it has never been washed. These items should be washed separately the first time to prevent ruining your other clothing.
- Separate your whites from the rest of your clothes. This will keep them from being affected by the other colours in your laundry, thus keeping them white.
- Separate your remaining light clothes from your dark clothes. Often the water temperature you will use is different according to the colour of the items being washed.

Pull out your laundry soap. You did bring soap, right? Take it out and look on the side of the box. Do you see the directions? Yes, there are directions! They are put there to help you choose what temperature you want your clothes washed in, and how much detergent or soap to use. Once you have completed

washing a few loads of laundry, you will begin to instinctively know how much soap to use and the temperature that is needed; for now, it is advisable for you to use the box as your guide. Generally, whites are washed in hot water, dark and coloured clothes in cold. If your load is smaller, set the water level guide on the machine to correspond, and use less soap.

Drying

Liquid fabric softeners are used in the rinse cycle of the wash. If your machine has an automatic fabric softener dispenser, you can put the liquid in there when you put the soap on the clothes — if not, you're going to have to wait around until the rinse cycle to add it directly to the water. An easier alternative for the beginner are fabric softener dryer sheets, which you put into the dryer along with the wet clothes. Not all clothes should go in the dryer — check the labels. Some things need to be hung dry because they have a tendency to fall apart or shrink. Lingerie and stockings should be washed inside a bag made for this purpose, which can be purchased at most department stores. Be sure to check all pockets for facial tissues or loose change or kleenex before washing or drying clothes.

Hand-washables should be done in cold water in the sink and hung to dry or dried flat. Use special soap designed for washing in cold water. Be sure to follow directions! Some things will even get damaged through hand-washing. Dry all sweaters flat, trying to retain their original shape — otherwise you will end up with elongated sleeves or a stretched neck.

Bleach

Only use regular chlorine bleach on whites, and follow the directions on the bottle carefully. Bleach not only whitens, it weakens fabrics, and can destroy them with over-use. Add regular chlorine bleach to wash water before adding clothes. New varieties of bleach for colours are also available, but are more expensive and should be used with caution. Again, follow the directions.

Ironing

You're probably going to need to buy an iron and an ironing board if you don't already have them. A steam iron is preferred, as it is easier to get the wrinkles out of things with steam than without. Don't use the steam setting for silk, however, as it will stain the fabric. A spray bottle is also useful for getting the wrinkles out of cotton shirts. Spray first, then iron. Be sure to check the settings on the iron and make sure they are appropriate for the fabric you are working on — a too-hot iron can melt or scorch some fabrics. Above all, be careful not to burn yourself, and make sure you unplug the iron when you're done.

Recycling

There was a time not so long ago when most individuals would not have understood what you meant when you told them to recycle. However, with the state that the Earth is presently in, it is not only necessary to understand, but to perform the duty of recycling every day. So, with this realization in mind, let's hit the garbage!

Depending upon what type of dwelling you are living in, either an apartment or townhome, you will be able to do either one or both of the following two things in relation to recycling:

- Recycle your garbage
- Composte your food waste

The principle behind recycling your garbage is to save the Earth from being cluttered with garbage, and to keep her resources from being over-used. Recycling is part of the three conservation R's: **Reduce, Reuse and Recycle.** After you have exhausted the first two possibilities, there are many things that are thrown into the garbage that can in fact be recycled. These items include:

- plastics
- paper
- tin
- glass

To save yourself the time of having to pick through your garbage every week, it is advisable to make yourself a "recycling box", if one is not available through your local recycling program.

Your recycling box can be as simple as a cardboard box in a closet where you throw items that can be reused or recycled. However, if it is going to become a permanent fixture in your home, it is wise to put some thought into how your recycling box will be constructed, and where it will be placed for the most convenience.

Your box can be constructed from almost any material. However, the best materials are those that are sturdy, and will handle heavy use. Cardboard is a material that stands up well to heavy use. If you have a few cardboard boxes in your home, find the largest one that will comfortably fit into the area you have chosen. If you don't have any boxes, a quick trip to your nearest grocery store will yield many to choose from.

Constructing your recycling box

- Obtain a box made of a sturdy material such as cardboard. Make sure it is of medium to large size, depending upon how much material you plan to recycle.
- Take a second box and use it for making compartments in your recycling box. Cut it up to fit inside your box, making at least four compartments: one for plastics, one for paper, one for tin and one for glass.
- If door-to-door service is not available in your area, inquire as to where the nearest recycling facility is located. This information can usually be obtained in your phone book in the Government section under Waste Management.
- Ask for recycling information to be sent to your home so that you are able to mark on your calendar the days that you must bring your items to be recycled, or prepare them for pick-up.
- Contact your community league to find out if there is a recycling program in effect in your community.

For those who live in townhomes or houses, your efforts do not need to be restricted to recycling. You can also eliminate throwing away your food refuse. All organic food items such as potato peelings, coffee grounds, egg shells or wilted lettuce can be put into a compost heap. This will not only cut down on your garbage, it will also put nutrients back into the soil.

Composting

To construct a composter, you will first need to find an area in your yard that is out of the way of traffic. If you are renting it is advisable to contact your resident manager to make sure composting is permitted in your complex. Once you have obtained permission and blocked off an area of your yard, you can begin construction!

First, you must decide between two composting options – you can make a compost bin (either do it yourself or ready-made) or you can make a compost pit.

The difference between the two is simply that a bin must either be constructed or bought, whereas a pit is just that, a pit you dig to put your compost in. If you choose to make a bin, please note that it should be a minimum of one metre square, and 1 to 1.6 metres high. The reason for this stipulation is that if its's any smaller, not enough heat may be generated inside to decompose the material efficiently. If it is higher, the compost on top may compress the material on the bottom, thus squeezing out the oxygen necessary to keep the process going.

Whether you have chosen a bin or a pit, the process for composting is the same. Just follow these easy steps, and you will be putting nutrients back into your garden in no time:

• Start with a layer of **coarse compost**. This can include the small branches pruned from your shrubs and trees, grass clippings, leaves or straw, just for example. Add to this first layer material such as good **garden soil, rotted manure, commercial compost mix** or **seaweed**, which is a very rich source of nutrients.

• Now, you are ready to add your first layer of **kitchen garbage**. All types of previous throw-away items such as wilted lettuce, eggshells, coffee grounds, tea leaves, fruit peels and even smaller pieces of paper are now ideal for your compost. And don't rule out things like lobster shells – just remember to break them up first as this helps them biodegrade more quickly.

• Also, to avoid visits from animals, it is best not to include meat or fish scraps, oil and grease, milk products or bones.
Now all that is left is to keep adding layers of soil, leaves, and kitchen garbage. Please keep in mind that if you are going to eat the garden produce that your compost is a part of, do not use any leaves or grass clippings that have been sprayed with pesticides or herbicides.

And there you have it! You have not only done your part to help clean up the Earth, but you have also helped to put vital nutrients back into it. You can now sleep at night with the knowledge that you have contributed to the planet. If you desire more information on composting and/or recycling in general, your local library can probably provide you with reading material that will give you this information.

Improving your quality of life

Let's see, one check goes to the rent, another goes to the utilities, another to cable, subtract that much for food, and the rest goes to decorating! What? This CAN'T be right, only this much for decorating? How am I supposed to make this place look half decent on this kind of money?

Many of us have faced, and are facing right now, this kind of problem. We have grand ideas of how we want our homes to look, and nowhere near the budget to meet these dreams. However, this does not mean that if your budget is limited, you can't slowly create the home you desire. It just takes some planning and a keen eye for bargains. There are some things that you should keep in mind when you begin to decorate you home. These include:

- Colour
- Space and scale
- Furniture arrangement

Now before you throw your hands up in despair, we will deal with each of these areas in a simple, straight forward manner that will give you the confidence to be your own interior decorator!

Decorating

As previously stated, we have three areas that need attention before we move into ideas for economical decorating. These areas can be best understood with some simple explanation, and the first one on our list is colour.

Colour

To some individuals, the issue of colour may seem straight forward. What is there to know besides making sure that your colours don't clash? Well, there are a couple of things:

- Use one, or just a few colours in a room. This not only achieves continuity, but also gives your room a sense of spaciousness.
- Be aware that bright, dramatic and contrasting colours on your walls and floors will tend to make your room seem closed-in. It is best to use colours that are low-keyed if you want to use several.
- Dark panelling will make your room seem darker and smaller. If possible, use a light paint or stain on your furniture that matches the wall surfaces. This will give a spacious effect to the room.

When dealing with colour, keep in mind that the more you limit yourself, the more unified your living space will seem.

Space and scale

Often the space available to you in an apartment or townhome is limited. Therefore, you must think carefully before adding any pieces of furniture or bricabrac to your rooms. Some considerations you might remember are:

- The size of your space is influenced by the visual space that an item takes up. Therefore, if your space is limited, consider using scaled-down pieces of furniture such as a love seat instead of a sofa. Also, smaller furniture will give you greater arrangement possibilities.

- When choosing furniture, try to find pieces that are space-saving. Examples of such items are wall storage units with fold-out tables, nesting tables, and tables that have separate leaves or a drop-leaf design.
- Any plants that you buy should not get in your way or cause you to have insufficient room to manoeuvre. Instead, they should accentuate the furniture and decorating that you have already done in the room. This means buying plants for spaces that you have designated just for them.

If you carefully consider the space available in each of the rooms that you plan to decorate, then you can keep a keen eye open for bargains on the more expensive items you may want. It is better to have slightly fewer of the decorating items you desire, than to have too many items that you don't care for cluttering up your space.

Furniture arrangement

The way in which you choose to arrange your furniture can have a great effect upon the apparent size, look and feel of a room. When arranging your furniture, keep in mind these suggestions:

- If you want to increase the apparent size of a room, place your furniture six inches or so away from the walls. This will create more flow around the furniture and a look that is more open. If you want to decrease the size of your space, then do the opposite: place furniture around the edges of the room.

- If your room has sloped ceilings, you might consider placing your furniture in a diagonal layout. This will create a larger space because of the area left around the furniture.
- If rooms such as the dining and living rooms have no division, you might consider using screens or other dividers to stop the flow of space between the two areas. Also, you can use your furniture, such as a love seat placed at a right angle to the wall, to divide the space.

As you can see, there are many ways to arrange your furniture to make maximum use of your space. The point to keep in mind is what look you are trying to achieve. Once you know the answer to this question, it is just a matter of time before you give your room the look you want.

Now that we have dealt with the three important areas of colour, space and scale, and arrangement, we can move onto some other ideas about where and how you can achieve your decorating goals.

Decorating ideas

Here is a quick list of ideas to help you along in your quest to find the furniture and other items you are looking for at economical prices.

- If your sofa and chairs are mis-matched and you can't afford to invest in new furniture, check your local department stores for inexpensive slip covers.
- If you have excess space that is too large for a plant, but too small for furniture, consider picking up some large pillows. These can become a comfortable item for your guests, and some may even prefer them to the other furniture in the room.

- Always be aware of where garage sales are being held. Often, just the item you have been staring at in an expensive store will be found at a garage sale, only in need of a little care to restore it to its original state.
- Consider making your own shelves. This can save money and be a great project as well. Scout around for some plywood and large bricks and grab a paint brush! Not only will you save money, but your own creation will give your room a uniqueness all its own.
- If your walls seem too barren and you don't want to clutter them with a bunch of nick-nacks, consider buying some hanging plants.

These are just a few suggestions to help you. After reading these, you might want to sit down with a pen and paper and see what kinds of ideas you can come up with on your own. Often, we just need some encouragement to find out what creative ideas we have lurking in the backs of our minds. So, open those minds and let those ideas loose! Give them lots of room to grow and help you to create the home that has been waiting in your dreams.

Food

Now that you've managed to create some semblance of normalcy in your new home, your next priority is food. After all, you have to eat — everything in the kitchen is nicely stored and you're hungry! Let's get something to eat.

Wise food shopping

Don't despair, you will not have to face the awesome task of shopping for food until you are briefed and ready! Once you have the necessary information, grocery shopping will not only be simple, but for some of you, it may also be a real adventure.

The first task before you is to divide your adventure into two parts; what to do before you get to the supermarket, and what to do when you are at the supermarket. Let's begin with part one.

Before you get to the supermarket

- Choose a grocery store. You may find that going to a few different supermarkets at first is the wisest decision. This enables you to compare them and decide which one best meets your needs.

- Check the newspaper for sales. It is advisable to check the papers for any sales and coupons you might be able to use to make your shopping more economical. Clip these items out and present them to the cashier when you are in the checkout line with the corresponding goods.
- Make a list. Making a list is important because individuals without them are the biggest targets for buying on impulse. If you have a list to follow, you are less inclined to pick up unnecessary items, and more inclined to get exactly what you need, and get through the checkout line quickly.
- Think about bringing your own reusable shopping bags to save wear and tear on the environment

At the supermarket

When you first walk through those automatic doors, your first inclination may be to walk right out again. Stop yourself before you do this — it's not as overwhelming as it seems. In fact, it's amazingly organized. Nice, neat rows of a isles with big signs above them to help direct you to where you want to go — kind of like a library. All you have to do is push your shopping cart along, choose your items and put them in the basket — a piece of cake! Let's see...lunch meat, bacon, wait a minute, what's all of this meat?! How am I supposed to choose which meat to buy when there are all these numbers and prices?

This is a common dilemma for most shoppers when they first start out. However, it's quite simple once you understand how meat is priced. The more meat, or weight there is in a package, the more it will cost you. It makes sense: the meat is weighed and then priced accordingly. Always be sure to check the unit price for what you are buying, be it meat or anything else. It will tell you how much the item costs per pound or kilogram. A higher price does not necessarily mean that the meat is better quality. Often, the most expensive meats are actually cheaper for you to buy per serving. Instead of buying more of a less expensive cut, it is wiser and healthier for you

to buy less of a higher quality cut. In this case, you are paying for the meat, not the excess fat and gristle that often accompanies the cheaper cut and increases its weight and price.

Once you have faced the intimidating meat counter, then the rest of your supermarket adventure is smooth sailing through the aisles ahead. Before heading off to the other aisles, however. check out the bulk sales.

Bulk sale items

Meat parts such as pork chops or chicken can be bought in bulk. Once you get your purchase home, you can divide it up into individual servings for freezing.

Dry goods are other popular items. Buying dry goods in bulk quantities is economical as these items are non-perishable and store very well. Some examples of dry goods include granola bars, pasta, nuts, spices and seasonings for cooking, items for baking, and so on.

Another important tip for supermarket shopping is to always buy non-perishable items in larger quantities. The unit price for these items is often considerably less when you buy the larger size. This is particularly so for items such as laundry soap and cleaning products, as well as paper goods.

You may have to store them longer, but they will save you money in the long run. If you are really ambitious about saving money, you may want to join a co-op or warehouse supermarket in your area, where larger quantities of goods are sold at close to wholesale prices.

Another important tip for you when you shop is to look for products that are recyclable, or are friendly to the environment, such as no-phosphate detergents and cleaners, or Enviro-pack containers. Avoid non-recyclables such as tetra juice packs.

Entertaining friends
on a budget

Let's see now, how much did I say I had for food this month? What, that can't be right! That's as bad as my decorating allowance! How am I going to entertain and feed my friends with this? Well, for entertainment I guess we could play charades, but they won't be laughing when instead of carrying out the food, I can only *mime* it!

The best way to celebrate your move into a new home is to have a house-warming party. But before you start looking up phone numbers, I have an even better idea. Let's first look at some easy and economical recipes that will give your friends and relatives an incentive to come over to your newly decorated home.

But where do I start? How do I entertain my friends on a budget, with the little knowledge of cooking that I have? Most singles, when first starting out, have to deal with the problem of entertaining on a budget. This does not mean, however, that you have to scratch the idea of ever having guests over to your home. It just means that you will have to do some careful budgeting to make sure that you don't over-extend yourself, and some scouting around for economical food recipes. To help you begin your quest for those delicious, yet economical, dishes, here are a few recipes to get you started.

Fruit Slush

(This can be made with or without the alcohol)

2 cups	apricot brandy	(500 mL)
1 cup	vodka or rum	(250 mL)
48oz. can	pineapple juice	(1.36 L)
48oz. can	apricot nectar	(1.36 L)
16oz. can	frozen orange juice	(474 mL)
1 16oz. can	frozen lemonade	(474 mL)

1) Mix together all of the ingredients in a large container that can be put in the freezer.
2) Freeze until slushy.
3) Serve 2 parts of the mixture to one part either 7-Up, Ginger-Ale, or Soda Water.
4) For a final touch, you can top each glass with a slice of lime.

This recipe serves 7.

Potato Skins

potatoes
bacon, cooked and crumbled
cheddar cheese, grated
melted butter
sour cream
green onion, thinly sliced

1) Scrub and prick potatoes.
2) Rub with oil and bake for 1 hour at 400° F; or until you are able to pierce potato easily. Once cooked let potatoes cool.

3) Slice potatoes in half lengthwise, then slice in half again. 4) Scoop out most of the potato , leaving a thin layer still on the skin.
5) Brush inside and outside of potatoes with butter and place vonto cookie sheet.
6) Bake at 500°F for 12 minutes or until potatoes are crisp.
7) Remove from oven and sprinkle generously with cheddar cheese and bacon.
8) Return to oven until cheese is melted.
9) Serve with sour cream and green onion as an option.

Cheese Fried Zucchini

1/4 cup dried	bread crumbs	(50 mL)
2 Tbsp.	grated parmesan cheese	(30 mL)
2 Tbsp.	flour	(30 mL)
1 tsp.	salt	(5 mL)
2	medium zucchini, sliced into sticks	
1	egg, beaten	
2-4 Tbsp.	oil or olive oil	(30-60 mL)

1) Combine bread crumbs, cheese, flour and salt in plastic bag.
2) Dip zucchini sticks in egg, shake in plastic bag mixture.
3) Fry in hot oil until golden brown and crispy. (Turn sticks occasionally.)
4) Drain on paper towel and serve immediately.

Yields 4 servings.

Broccoli Soup

2 10 oz. packages	chopped frozen broccoli	(567 g)
1/4 cup	onion, finely chopped	(50 mL)
2 cups	chicken broth	(500 mL)
2 Tbsp.	butter	(30 mL)
1 Tbsp.	flour	(15 mL)
1 tsp.	salt	(5 mL)
	pepper to taste	
2 cups	half & half cream	(500 mL)

1) Thaw broccoli. Combine with onion and broth. (Option: save a few broccoli "trees" for garnish).
2) Bring mixture to a boil. Reduce heat and simmer for 10 minutes.
3) For a smooth consistency, pour mixture into a blender.
4) Melt butter in a large saucepan, add flour, salt, and pepper.
5) Slowly add the cream, stirring until smooth.
6) Add broccoli and warm to serving temperature.
7) Garnish with broccoli "trees."

Yield 4 servings.

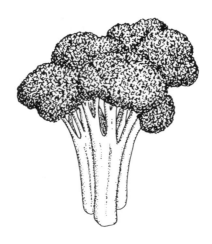

Hot Mushroom Salad

1/2 cup	*Olive oil*	*(125 mL)*
1/4 cup	*Tarragon vinegar*	*(50 mL)*
2-3 tsps	*dijon mustard*	*(30-45 mL)*
1 clove	*minced garlic*	
	salt and pepper to taste	
1 head	*butter lettuce, torn into bite sized pieces*	
1/4 lb.	*monterey jack cheese, shredded*	*(115 g)*
1/2 lb.	*fresh mushrooms*	*(250 g)*
2 Tbsps	*butter*	*(30 mL)*

1) In a screw top jar, combine oil, vinegar, mustard, garlic,salt and pepper. Shake well.
2) Place salad plates in freezer for at least one hour.
3) Mix torn lettuce, cheese and dressing in a bowl.
4) Place mixture on the cold salad plates.
5) Immediately saute mushrooms until very hot and spoon over salad. (Hot mushrooms should melt cheese.)

Yields 4 servings.

Oat-bran Muffins

1 cup	flour	(250 mL)
1 tsp.	baking powder	(5 mL)
1 tsp.	baking soda	(5 mL)
1/2 tsp.	salt	(2.5 mL)
1 cup	raisins	(250 mL)
1 cup	oat bran	(250 mL)
1 cup	heavy cream	(250 mL)
1/3 cup	oil	(80 mL)
3 Tbsps	corn syrup	(45 mL)
1	egg	
1/4 cup	brown sugar	(60 mL)
1/2 tsp.	vanilla	(2 1/2 mL)

Preheat your oven to 375°F.
1) In a medium-sized mixing bowl, combine together the flour, baking powder, baking soda, salt and raisins.
2) In a small mixing bowl, soak the oat bran in the cream for 5 minutes.
3) Add the oil, corn syrup, egg, sugar and vanilla, and pour mixture into dry ingredients.
4) Beat mixture for 2 minutes. The batter should be lumpy.
5) Grease 12 muffin tins and pour batter into tins to 2/3 full.
6) Bake for 20 to 25 minutes.

Makes 12 muffins.

Whole Wheat Bread

3/4 cup	milk	(175 mL)
1/4 cup	firmly packed brown sugar	(50 mL)
1 Tbsp.	salt	(15mL)
1/3 cup	butter	(80mL)
1/3 cup	molasses	(80mL)
1 1/2 cups	lukewarm water	(375mL)
2 packages	yeast	
6 cups	stone-groundwhole-wheat flour	(1.5L)
1	egg wash	

(**Egg wash:** egg white and 1 tsp. salt. Combine egg white and salt; beat with fork until foamy.)

1) Scald milk in saucepan, add brown sugar, salt, butter, and molasses.
2) Stir mixture until dissolved; let stand until lukewarm.
3) Pour lukewarm water into large, warm, mixing bowl.
4) Sprinkle yeast over water and stir until dissolved.
5) Pour in milk mixture, stirring constantly. Stir in 4 cups of whole-wheat flour, 1 cup at a time, mixing until smooth. Stir in remaining whole-wheat flour.
6) Sprinkle counter top with flour and knead dough for 10 minutes, or until your dough is smooth and elastic.
7) Knead in remaining flour.
8) Place dough into a well-buttered bowl; making sure the top of dough is greased too. Cover with a towel and let rise in a warm place for 1 hour; or until dough is double in bulk.
9) Divide dough in half and turn onto lightly-floured surface.
10) Knead again and shape halves into loaves. Place in two greased 9x5 inch loaf pans.
11) Cover and let rise in warm place until double in bulk.
12) Bake at 400°F for ten minutes.
13) Brush with egg wash and bake another 15 minutes.

Makes 2 (9x5 inch) loaves.

Onion and Beef Stew

1 1/4 pounds	stew beef, cut into 1 inch pieces	(550 g)
1/4 cup	olive oil	(60 mL)
2 cups	sliced onions	(500 mL)
2 cloves	minced garlic	
1/2 tsp.	salt	(2 mL)
1/2 tsp.	pepper	(2 mL)
1/2 tsp.	allspice	(2 mL)
1 (2 inch) piece	cinnamon stick	
1 1/4 cups	dry red wine	(310 mL)
1 (8oz.) can	tomato sauce	(225 g)

1) Brown beef in hot oil, remove from pan.
2) Brown onions and garlic, add remaining ingredients and stir well.
3) Add beef to mixture and bring to a boil.
4) Reduce heat to simmer; cover.
5) Cook, stirring occasionally for approximately 2 hours or until meat is very tender.

Yields 4 servings.

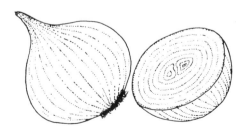

6	*pork chops*	
1 (8oz.)can	*mushrooms; sliced and drained*	*(225 g)*
1/4 cup	*finely chopped onions*	*(60 mL)*
2 tbsp.	*butter*	*(30 mL)*
2 tbsp.	*flour*	*(30 mL)*
1 1/2 tsp.	*salt*	*(7 mL)*
1 tsp.	*curry powder*	*(5 mL)*
1 1/2 cups	*milk*	*(375 mL)*

1) Trim excess fat from pork chops and brown lightly on both sides in frying pan.
2) Place in a baking pan and cover with mushrooms.
3) Cook onion in butter until tender.
4) Stir in flour, salt, and curry powder.
5) Add milk, stirring in gradually.
6) Cook, stirring constantly, until thickened.
7) Pour mixture over chops and cover pan.
8) Bake in preheated 350°F oven for 1 hour; or until pork chops are tender.

Yields 6 servings.

Asparagus Quiche

1 lb.	*asparagus*	*(435 g)*
2 Tbsps	*soft butter*	*(30 mL)*
1/4 cup	*fine, dry breadcrumbs*	*(50 mL)*
8 slices	*bacon,*	
or 1 cup	*diced cooked ham*	*(250 mL)*
1 cup	*grated cheddar cheese*	*(250 mL)*
3	*eggs, beaten*	
1 cup	*light cream*	*(250 mL)*
1/2 cup	*milk*	*(125 mL)*
	pinch nutmeg	
	freshly ground pepper	

1) Cut asparagus into 2 inch lengths.
2) Cook in boiling salted water until tender-crisp. Drain well.
3) Spread bottom and sides of a 10-inch quiche dish with the butter.
4) Sprinkle the breadcrumbs on top and make sure bottom and sides of dish are coated.
5) Cook bacon until crisp, drain and crumble. Sprinkle over the crumbs. Sprinkle 3/4 cup of cheese over bacon.
6) Arrange asparagus over cheese, reserving 6 of the tips for the top.
7) Beat eggs, cream, milk and seasonings and pour over all.
8) Top with rest of the cheese.
9) Decorate top with reserved asparagus tips.
10) Bake at 350°F for 40-45 minutes.

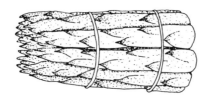

Green Beans and Mushrooms

1 lb.	*frozen french-cut green beans*	*(435 g)*
1 can	*sliced mushrooms, drained*	
1 can	*mushroom soup*	
1/2 cup	*milk or cream*	*(125 mL)*
1 cup	*breadcrumbs*	*(250 mL)*
2 Tbsps	*butter*	*(30 mL)*
1/2 cup	*parmesan cheese*	*(125 mL)*
	salt and pepper to taste	

1) Cook frozen beans according to package instructions, just until tender-crisp.
2) Grease a 1 1/2 quart casserole.
3) Mix beans with mushrooms, and mushroom soup which has been thinned with the cream or milk, salt and pepper.
4) Place all in casserole and top with crumbs.
5) Bake at 350°F for 45 minutes, or until heated through.

Makes 6 servings

Crumb topping:
1) Melt 2 Tbsps butter in frying pan.
2) Add 1 cup breadcrumbs and 1/2 cup of parmesan cheese.

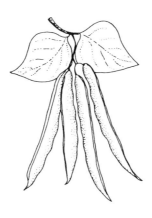

**Apple Juice
Chicken Surprise**

1 cup	*flour*	*(250 mL)*
2 tsps	*salt*	*(10 mL)*
1/4 tsp.	*pepper*	*(1 mL)*
3-4 lbs.	*chicken; cut-up*	*(1.5-2 kg)*
1/4 cup	*melted butter*	*(50 mL)*
4	*chopped green onions*	
1/2 cup	*sliced mushrooms*	*(125 mL)*
2 tbsps	*lemon juice*	*(30 mL)*
1 tsp.	*sugar*	*(5 mL)*
1 tsp.	*salt*	*(5 mL)*
1/3 cup	*apple juice*	*(75 mL)*

1) Combine flour, salt, and pepper in a plastic bag. Place chicken in bag, shake well to coat.
2) Brown chicken in butter and remove to casserole dish.
3) Add green onions and mushrooms to frying pan. Cover and simmer for 3 minutes. Add to casserole dish.
4) Mix together lemon juice, sugar, salt and apple juice.
5) Pour over chicken and bake at 325°F for 1 hour.

Yields 6 servings.

1 lb.	lean ground beef	(435 g)
1	medium onion, chopped	
1/2 cup	milk	(125 mL)
1	egg, beaten	
8	crushed soda crackers	
	salt and pepper to taste	
1/4 cup	ketchup	(50 mL)
1/4 cup	water	(50 mL)
1 tsp.	dry mustard	(5 mL)
1/2 cup	brown sugar	(125 mL)

1) Combine ground beef, onion, milk, egg, crackers, salt and pepper; mix well.
2) Place in an 8x4x3 loaf pan; make a groove down the centre of loaf.
3) In a bowl, combine ketchup, water, mustard, and brown sugar.
4) Pour over meat and bake at 350°F for 1 hour; drain.
Yields 4-6 servings.

1 can	mandarin oranges, drained	
1	apple, peeled and sliced	
1	banana, sliced,	
	sprinkled with lime or lemon juice	
6	dates, cut in half	
1/4 cup	chopped walnuts	(60 mL)

Combine all fruit in a glass bowl and sprinkle with walnuts.

4-6	*tart apples*	*(medium sized)*
2 1/2	*lemons, juiced*	
3 Tbsps	*sugar*	*(45 mL)*
3 Tbsps	*butter*	*(45 mL)*
3/4 cup	*sugar*	*(175 mL)*
2	*eggs, separated*	
1 tsp.	*baking powder*	*(5 mL)*
1 1/2 cups	*flour*	*(375 mL)*
3/4 cup	*milk*	*(175 mL)*
1 Tbsp.	*rum*	*(15 mL)*
1 tsp.	*butter (to grease pan)*	*(5 mL)*
1 tsp.	*vegetable oil*	*(5 mL)*
3 tsps	*powdered sugar*	*(45 mL)*

1) Peel the apples, cut them in half and core. Cut decorative slits in the apple halves approximately 1/2 inch deep.
2) Sprinkle them with lemon juice and 3 Tbsps of sugar; now set aside.
3) Cream together 3/4 cup of sugar and butter. Beat in egg yolks one at a time, and gradually beat in the lemon juice and grated peel.
4) Sift together flour and baking powder; gradually add mixture to butter and sugar batter. Blend in milk and rum.
5) In a separate, small bowl, beat egg whites until stiff; fold into batter.
6) Grease a springform pan generously. Pour in batter and top with prepared apple halves. Brush the apples with vegetable oil.
7) Bake in a preheated 350°F oven for 35 to 40 minutes. Remove from pan and sprinkle with powdered sugar.

Yields 6 servings.

1 3/4 cups	*unsifted flour*	*(375 mL)*
1 Tbsp.	*baking powder*	*(15 mL)*
1/2 tsp.	*salt*	*(2 mL)*
3/4 cup	*sugar*	*(175 mL)*
1/2 cup	*shortening or butter*	*(125 mL)*
2	*eggs*	
1 cup	*mashed bananas*	*(250 mL)*

Preheat your oven to 350°F and grease a 9 x 5-inch pan.

1) Mix together thoroughly flour. baking powder and salt.
2) Mix together sugar, butter, and eggs until light and fluffy,
   then mix in the bananas. Add dry ingredients and stir just
   until smooth.
3) Pour batter into greased and floured pan.
4) Bake until firmly set when touched lightly in centre tops,
   approximately 50-60 minutes. (It is possible that the bread
   may crack across the top.)
5) Allow to cool on rack, and remove from baking pan after 10
   minutes.

Rice Pudding Deluxe

2 cups	cooked rice	(500 mL)
1/2 tsp.	salt	(2 mL)
1 (20 oz.) can	crushed pineapple, drained	625 mL)
1/2 pint	whipped cream, beaten stiff	(250 mL)

1) Mix together rice, salt, and pineapple until well blended.
2) Reserving some for garnish, gently fold in most of whipped cream.
3) Spoon mixture into individual serving dishes; top with reserved whipped cream.

Yield 6-8 servings.

Baked Custard

3 cups	milk	(750 mL)
4	eggs	
1/3 cup	sugar	(90 mL)
1/4 tsp.	salt	(1 mL)
1 tsp.	vanilla	(5 mL)
	Nutmeg or cinnamon (optional)	

1) Heat milk until hot (not boiling).
2) Beat eggs in large bowl.
3) Add sugar and salt.
4) Add milk slowly, stirring continually.
5) Mix in vanilla and pour into baking pan.
6) Sprinkle with nutmeg or cinnamon.
7) Bake at 300°F for approximately 1 hour, or until a knife stuck into centre comes out clean.

Makes 6 servings.

Creamy Fruit Salad

1 (8 oz.) package	cream cheese	(225 g)
1 Tbsp.	syrup from canned mandarin oranges	(15 mL)
1 (11 oz.) can	mandarin orange sections, drained	(310 g)
1 (13 1/2 oz.) can pineapple tidbits, drained		(380 g)
1 cup	miniature marshmallows	(250 mL)
1/3 cup	halved, drained, maraschino cherries	(90 mL)
	Iceberg lettuce	

1) Beat softened cream cheese with liquid from mandarin oranges until creamy.
2) Add oranges, pineapple, and marshmallows; combine thoroughly.
3) Lightly fold in cherries; chill.
4) Serve in a small dessert bowl lined with lettuce.

Makes 6 servings.

Your Favourite Recipes

Your Favourite Recipes

Your Favourite Recipes

What's Next?

Whew! Now there are a few recipes to get you started! These are just a few selections to get you going in the right direction, the rest is up to you. Your friends and family will be impressed by your cooking talents, and maybe they will feel compelled to return the favour and invite you to their homes!

But don't stop here! We'd like to recommend that you stock up on some basic cookbooks like "The Joy of Cooking", or take some cooking classes offered through your local public school system or University. Don't think you're the only one who's never cooked or ironed before! There are lots of new singles out there who need help in learning these basic life skills. Where there's a need, there is usually a book or a class. So don't be shy! Try your local public library and do some reading on the topics we introduced you to here. There are many books available on decorating, cooking, storage, etc. that you will find useful besides this one.

We at Homeworld wish you "clear sailing," and hope to help you along in alternate areas that you desire to gain knowledge of in the future. What's that? Did you say creamy fruit salad? I'll be right over!

OTHER HOMEWORLD TITLES

ATTRACTING BIRDS

ISBN 0-919433-87-1   64 pp.   5 1/2 x 8 1/2 $6.95

NORTHERN BALCONY GARDENING

ISBN 0-919433-98-7   64 pp.   5 1/2 x 8 1/2 $6.95

JAMS AND JELLIES

ISBN 0-919433-90-1   48 pp.   5 1/2 x 8 1/2 $4.95

PICKLES AND PRESERVES

ISBN 0-919433-88-X   48 pp.   5 1/2 x 8 1/2 $4.95

HERBS FOR NORTHERN GARDENERS

ISBN 0-919433-99-5   64 pp.   5 1/2 x 8 1/2 $6.95

CANADIAN HERITAGE BREADMAKING

ISBN 1-55105-016-1   64 pp.   5 1/2 x 8 1/2 $6.95

CHRISTMAS SURVIVAL GUIDE

ISBN 1-55105-019-6   64 pp.   5 1/2 x 8 1/2 $6.95

FURNITURE REFINISHING MADE EASY

ISBN 1-55105-022-6   64 pp.   5 1/2 x 8 1/2 $6.95

Look for these and other Lone Pine books at your local bookstore. If they're unavailable, order direct from:

Lone Pine Publishing
#206 10426-81 Avenue
Edmonton, Alberta   T6E 1X5
Phone: (403) 433-9333   Fax: (403) 433-9646